Spelling Strategies That Work

Practical Ways to Motivate Successful Spellers

by Min Hong and Patsy Stafford

S C H O L A S T I C
PROFESSIONAL BOOKS

New York ◆ Toronto ◆ London ◆ Auckland ◆ Sydney

To my parents, Inja and Sang Seol,
for encouraging me to dream.
— M. H.

To my first teachers, my parents—
Pat and Bet.
— P. S.

Special thanks to Liza Charlesworth, Wendy Murray, Jaime Lucero,
and Susan Shafer at Scholastic; our colleagues at PS 11;
and most of all, our first- and second-grade writers at PS 11.

Cover design by Kathy Massaro.
Cover photography by Andrew Levine.
Interior design by Jaime Lucero and Liza Charlesworth for Graphica, Inc.
All photos courtesy of the authors except page 9 © copyright Andrew Levine.

TABLE OF CONTENTS

INTRODUCTION

Our beliefs and strategies for teaching young children to spell evolved over time. Essentially, they're a result of two factors: our personal experiences as children and our observations of children in our classrooms. Although we're two teachers who come from different backgrounds, we share similar experiences in this area. Our stories follow:

I came to the U.S.A. from Seoul, Korea when I was seven years old. I'll never forget my first experience entering school. It was Friday morning. I was given a piece of paper to take the weekly spelling test. I didn't know how to speak English, let alone know how to write my name, and yet I was asked to participate in taking a spelling test. I sat and watched as other children wrote frantically.

On Monday, when I entered my classroom, there on my desk was a piece of paper. As I sat down, I turned over the paper, only to see a big red 0. Soon I understood what the teacher wanted me to do. She wanted me to memorize a list of words. Eventually, I knew the tricks of getting a "100" on spelling tests. However, I never really learned how certain words are spelled, and, to this day, I struggle in taking risks in that area.

This experience was a big factor in my developing alternative ways to teach spelling. Throughout my elementary years, my classmates and I were discouraged from writing about personal experiences in school, experiences that were important to us. In particular, I remember wanting to write a story in class about my grandmother coming from Korea to visit our family here in the United States. But my teacher said there wasn't time to write about that topic in class. Perhaps I'd like to write about it when I got home? After all, in class we were busy completing assignments, mostly in workbooks. (In fact, every subject was taught with workbooks!)

There was another stumbling block to writing a story in class: I didn't know how to spell some of the words pertaining to my subject (such as celebrate or holiday). If a word wasn't on the class spelling list, how would I know how to write it? For all these reasons, I was reluctant to write.
During writing time in class, we kids were given a beginning sen-

tence, asked to finish it, and build a story from it. When I was finished with my work, I'd line up at my teacher's desk, where she was sitting, and get my story "checked." Back at my own desk, I'd look at my paper and see red marks around misspelled words, with the conventional spelling written above them. My teacher assumed that once I had seen the conventional spelling, I'd remember how to spell the "correct way." If I misspelled a word again, I had to write it ten times.

This type of teaching led me to believe that I wasn't a writer. I found myself detouring around creative stories because I was afraid to take a chance with words I wasn't quite sure how to spell. Instead, I wrote the same stories over and over again, using words I already knew. Basically, I had two choices: write creatively and make spelling errors, or write familiar stories using known words and avoid seeing red marks all over my paper.

— Min Hong

Growing up in Ireland, with eight siblings who went to the same three-room school house and had the same teachers as I did, I often wondered why some of my siblings had such a hard time learning to spell. Writing in the early grades involved copying the teacher's written words. You could not begin to compose your own writing until you had learned to spell words; even then, writing was limited to the words that you knew how to spell. Incorrect spelling was frowned upon, and the teacher used her red pen liberally to indicate mistakes. Words that were misspelled had to be written ten times to ensure you would not make the same mistake again.

Every Friday, we had a spelling test. The night before, my mother would help us kids to memorize our words. And she would test us the next morning before school. Unfortunately, my younger brothers always got the words wrong on the actual test. My mother would say, "But you knew them this morning. What happened?" (Evidently, they memorized the words at night but went blank the day of the test. The stress of the test threw them off.) My brothers came to accept that they were "bad" spellers. As a visual learner, I had few *problems learning my spelling words and could always visualize how a word should look.*

When I began teaching and thought back to my early years, I realized that there were lots of children like my brothers who couldn't learn to spell the traditional way. I began to look for alternative ways to teach spelling that would meet all children's needs. By the way, my three siblings are still poor spellers today, but have learned to compensate by using dictionaries and spell checks.

— Patsy Stafford

As we gained experience as teachers, we realized that a set spelling list would not meet the needs of every child. While some children need help forming plurals, others still struggle with basic letter sounds. A class list would be too hard for some children and unchallenging for others. We also realized that children often know how to spell correctly on a test (because they have memorized the words) but are unable to transfer that knowledge to their writing.

With these realizations in mind, we have integrated spelling into every aspect of our literacy programs. In our classrooms, there is no single spelling list or set time or day to take a test. Rather, spelling is individualized to meet the needs of each child.

We have been fortunate to work at the same school for the last four years. During that time, we've talked with each other about how we teach spelling, sharing our ideas and strategies. Because about half of Min's first graders go on to Patsy's class in second grade, we decided to combine our spelling programs to create one that provides kids with a consistent approach in each grade. As a starting point, we looked at our past and present practices (see chart on page 7).

This comparison took us to the next step. We decided to closely study the learning styles of four children over a two-year period (through first and second grades). This research helped validate for us our sense that each child has a different way of learning how to spell. Although direct teaching through small groups and whole groups is vital, we felt that we must keep in sight the individual child's ability to spell. To this day, we continue to ask questions and take careful notes on each child's learning style.

In our district, many staff developers see our classrooms as places to send other teachers to learn our techniques. They ask many questions, and we spend a lot of time explaining the role the teaching of spelling has in an Integrated Language Arts classroom. Because their response was so favorable, we decided to share our approach with others by writing this book.

THE WAY WE WERE TAUGHT	THE WAY WE TEACH
◆ One list for everyone	◆ More individualized lists
◆ Arbitrary list of grade-appropriate words	◆ Words from children's writing – No limit on words kids learn
◆ Friday spelling test	◆ Peer testing – Children work with partners and teacher to check knowledge of words
◆ One strategy – Rote memorization	◆ Lots of strategies – Prior knowledge – Environmental print – Word patterns – Visual memory – Auditory memory
◆ Spelling taught as isolated lesson/activity	◆ Spelling integrated throughout day, taught in context
◆ Kids use only words they know	◆ Kids take risks
◆ Teachers corrected children's spelling in red ink	◆ Children self-edit with peer or teacher assistance
◆ Grading	◆ No grading
◆ No encouragement for close approximation	◆ Encouragement to "Have a Go"
◆ Getting help from a friend was considered cheating	◆ Peers help each other with spelling words

In *Spelling Strategies That Work,* we share what works well with *our* children. We don't see it as the *only* way. Being classroom teachers gives us insight into long-term individual learning that a researcher visiting a classroom for a day or two doesn't have. After all, working with our children since the first day of school gives us a knowledge of the children's learning styles, their home situations, and their progress throughout the year.

We feel a professional book written by two classroom teachers who "practice what they preach" is powerful and meaningful. We hope this book will become a practical tool for you as you develop a spelling program in your own classroom.

What Makes a Good Speller?

My name is KiKi.
I live in New York City.
I like writing about myself.
Cause typing and writing is fun!
Do you think typing and writing is fun?
I like writing and typing because you get to write anything you want.
So now do you have any ideas to write about?
Oh well I guess that you will think about it.
I make up stories when I don't have anymore true stuff to write about.
So you can make up stories too!
And now do you have any ideas?
Well that's okay. So I hope that you like writing and typing now.
Oh yeah! I forgot to tell you something do not worrie about spelling!
Because you soon will learn to spell.
And you will be able to correct your spelling!
So farewell my friends!

A second-grade child typed this story about writing during computer class.

Conditions of Learning

As we thought about what needs to happen for children to become good spellers, we thought of Brian Cambourne's seven conditions of learning.[1] Here, we've listed each condition, along with a photo and caption showing the relevance to our classroom practice.

1. Cambourne, Brian (1988). *The Whole Story.* New York: Scholastic.

CAMBOURNE'S SEVEN CONDITIONS OF LEARNING

1. Immersion

Children need to be immersed in the written word. They need to see conventional spelling around them on charts, books, posters, and so forth.

An illustrated rendition of a poem by Lois Lenski hangs in the room, celebrating first graders' New York City social studies curriculum.

For a study of logos, first graders displayed their growing collection.

2. Demonstration

Children need to see correct spelling and its process demonstrated. They need to see modeling of the writing and editing process.

Patsy and her students compose a story about their visit to the Transit Museum.

3. Engagement

Children use what they have learned in real life.

Encouraged to be aware of environmental print, Naida, a first grader, sorted through the library for poetry books and made signs for the baskets.

4. Expectation

There needs to be an expectation that children will write and that they will edit their work. Children are aware of what they are capable of doing.

Min and her first graders developed a writing rubric to help kids become aware of the characteristics of good writing.

5. Responsibility

Children need to be expected to take responsibility for their learning. They need to be involved in the decision making surrounding their learning.

After conferencing, Tyrell, a first grader, rereads his piece to make changes.

6. Response/Feedback

Children need to receive responses and feedback from teacher and peers.

After sharing his published book, John listens to responses from his teacher and classmates.

7. Approximation

Children are encouraged to take risks so that they may discover their own learning.

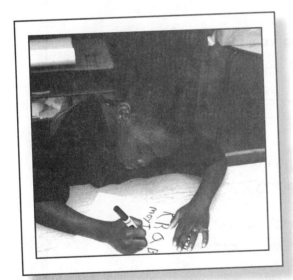

During "free choice" time, Tyrell explores writing on his own.

What Should a Spelling Program Include?

Often, we talk to our children about what they can do when they're at home and not sure how to spell a word (look it up in a dictionary, find it in another book, ask someone, sound it out). These discussions encourage children to use a variety of resources to spell words in their daily lives.

We also encourage children to be equally resourceful in the classroom, and consequently we often find children consulting various resources when they want to spell words.

For example, if you walk into either of our classrooms during work centers workshop, you might notice that one child is looking up a spelling in her personal word book, while another child pauses in her work in the block area to find the word *zoo* on the word wall. (She's writing a label for her block-building project.) The print-rich environment we have created allows children to use various areas of the room to find the correct spelling of all sorts of words.

PRINCIPLES

Some of the basic tenets that guide our work with children are:

- The teaching of spelling has to be individualized to meet each student's needs.

- Spelling words should be selected from the children's own writing so that they are relevant, not just an isolated list of words.

- Teaching spelling needs to be integrated into every aspect of the classroom, not just writing.

- Children need a variety of strategies and tools for figuring out how a word is spelled and for editing incorrectly spelled words.

- Children need to be comfortable taking risks with invented spelling so that they don't rely on sight words only.

- Learning to spell is a process.

What Do Good Spellers Do?

When we talked with our colleagues about developing an effective spelling program, the first question we asked ourselves was: "What does a good speller do?" We knew that the answer to this question would help us develop a sound program that would reach all the learners in our classes. In addition, we "kid-watched" carefully, jotting down notes about how good spellers go about their work.

As a result of these efforts, we discovered that successful spellers:
- are risk takers.
- use patterns.
- are avid readers.
- are prolific writers.

We also found that good spellers:
- use visual and phonetic knowledge.
- have a good idea of how a word should look.
- know common spelling patterns, letter positions, and letter frequency.
- have strategies for figuring out the correct spelling of a word.
- know what resources to use to edit their spelling.

We then asked our first and second graders, "What do good spellers do?" Here are their responses:

I'm a good speller. If I don't know, I just spell it out, and when I hear the words, I put the letter down where I hear the words.

A good speller is someone who practices. A good speller is someone who writes every day. A good speller is someone who asks for words.

Chapter 2

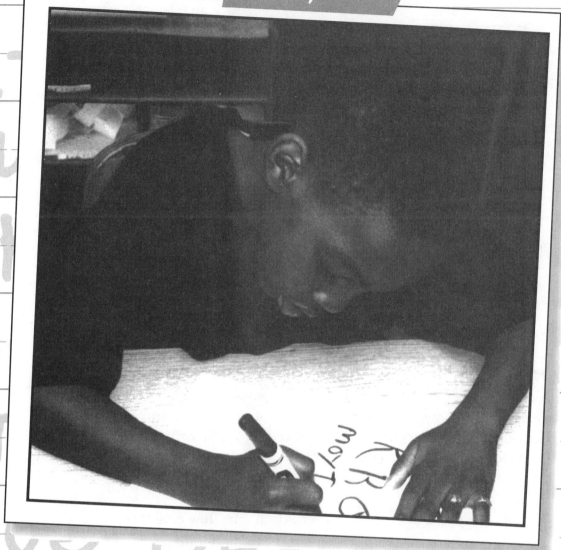

Creating a Writing Workshop:

The Foundations of Spelling & Phonics

photo credit: Sheila Callaghan

Second graders engage in writing workshop.

Creating a Language-Rich Environment

As we moved toward using alternative ways to teach spelling, we began to design a language-rich environment that supported our goal that students become independent-minded readers and writers. We gave careful consideration to the layout and the setup of our rooms, asking ourselves some new but crucial questions:

◆ Is the room set up so that children can flow easily between centers?

◆ Are materials—from finger paints to dictionaries—easily accessible?

◆ Do children know where materials are stored?

◆ Do children know how to use the materials?

A few weeks into the school year, we spend time teaching children how to use materials (such as the date stamp and stapler) and where to find materials (such as paper, pencils, and journals). This ensures a smooth work time throughout the year.

Though our schedules change somewhat from day to day, we try to schedule reading and writing back-to-back (see photo on page 19). After all, we reasoned, reading and writing are interrelated, so it's a natural transition to go from one to the other. In particular, our mini-lessons on writing or spelling often relate to the books the children are reading, which is also reflected in what they choose to write about. Reading and writing go hand-in-hand.

The schedule of the day helps our kids know what to expect during the day. Notice that reading workshop and writing workshop are back-to-back.

Mini-Lessons

Our mini-lessons are direct teaching times when we focus on the skills and strategies necessary to become good readers, writers, and spellers. The mini-lessons may involve the whole class, a small group, or an individual who has a specific need. Before children go off to read or write, we use the beginning workshop time to talk about a skill or strategy that may help them. For example, if we noticed that many children in class were forgetting to add *s* for plural, we might do a whole chart of plural words ending in *s*. However, if only one child needed help in that area, we would teach it to that child individually.

Extending Lessons

We use trade books, children's writing, our own personal writing, and charts to demonstrate. The charts that we create are displayed around the room so that children can refer to or add to them later. We ask children to be aware during the day of words that relate to something we taught earlier. For example, if we focused on the *long a* sound in a morning lesson, we ask children to search for words that have that sound during the rest of the day and then to add those words to the charts.

How do we decide what spelling lessons to teach? Many spelling mini-lessons develop by looking at children's writing during individual conference time. In first grade, children often write stories using all uppercase letters. Frequently, they forget to leave spaces between words. In second grade, children learn about sentences and punctuation marks. These are good topics for mini-lessons.

Tina's story about her new house. We might use it to teach a mini-lesson on leaving spaces between words.

A Mini-Lesson Revealed

One day during individual conferences, I (Min) noticed that three out of five children needed work on the *ed* ending. The next morning, before writing workshop started, I did a mini-lesson on the *ed* ending, using a child's story.

> I went to the park yesterday. I showd off to my mom I coold do the monkee bar. She sid, "WOW." Then I halpt my littl sistr do the monkee bar. We got tird so mommy took us hom.

Teacher: I noticed yesterday that Aisha was doing something interesting as a speller. So I asked permission to use her writing for our mini-lesson today. Aisha, would you please read your story to us? (The story is reproduced on a transparency, then placed on an overhead projector.)

Aisha: (She reads her story.)

Teacher: As I look at Aisha's writing, I see that she really has been working hard on her spelling. But yesterday, during writing conferences, I noticed that she and some other children were having the same problem. So, today we are going to look at words that end in *ed*. Look at Aisha's story. Does anyone notice which words may end with *ed*?

Brian: *Could.*

Teacher: I see why you might think the word *could* would have an *ed* ending. Is it because it ends with a *d*?

Brian: (Nods.)

Teacher: That's good thinking. But the word *could* doesn't end in *ed*. Usually a word ending in *ed* means it's past tense. Does anyone think they know what past tense means?

Sue: It means it already happened?

Teacher: Great. So does anyone else see a word ending in *ed*?

Eric: How about *showd* (*showed*)?

Teacher: That's great. Let's put it on a chart. Which letter is missing from *showd*? (Teacher writes *show_d*.)

Chorus: *E*. You can't hear the *e*.

I continued the mini-lesson, adding more *ed* words to the chart. However, when I pointed to *halpt* (*helped*) in Aisha's story, the children didn't realize that it should end in *ed*. Like Aisha, they all heard the word *helped* with the *t* as an ending. So I ended the mini-lesson by pointing out that when we sound out words, it's helpful to say the word slowly to ourselves. Saying *helped* slowly diminishes the *t* sound you might hear when the word is said fast, in conversation. I kept the list of *ed* words in front of the room. Throughout the week, during reading and writing time, children added words to it. Later, as I reflected on the lesson, I realized that Aisha also struggled with *silent e* words. Therefore, for her next individual conference, I planned to focus on the *silent e* words.

(For a list of other mini-lessons we teach, see the chart on page 23.)

Writing Workshop

After a mini-lesson, we distribute writing folders or journals, and the whole class begins to write individual stories. We begin with five minutes of silent writing. That period of quiet time helps children focus on their writing. Noise or interruptions may distract them, preventing them from starting or concentrating on their work. (As the year progresses, we extend silent time to ten or fifteen minutes.) After silent time, the children may choose to confer with classmates, ask for spelling help, read their stories aloud, or work with a partner on creating a book.

While the class is writing, we confer with and assess individual children. You may want to have children join you at a table, or you may want to circulate around the room and give "on-the-spot" assistance.

It's important to jot down key notes during conference time. We use a variety of forms to record assessment notes, such as grids and labels (see the sample on page 24). We collect these forms in a binder, or in individual files, to make it easier for us to refer to past assessment notes or to measure progress or growth. (Please see Chapter 5 for more on conferencing and assessment.)

We thought it would be helpful for you to get a sense of some of the supplies in our writing centers.

What's in a writing center:

WRITING CENTER SUPPLIES

- Trays or baskets of different types of paper (lined, blank, colored, etc.)
- Dictionaries
- Stationery with envelopes
- Notepads and sticky notes
- Alphabet charts
- Journals and folders
- Crayons, markers, and pencils

- Date stamps
- Stapler, tape, rulers, and scissors
- Clipboards
- Book-publishing supplies
- Computer and printer
- Word Wall
- Displays of children's writing
- Basket of children's original books

Min has a formal conference with each child on a regular basis. As part of her record keeping, she jots down quick notes on labels as she interacts with her students.

MIGUEL: Still writing strings of letters. Getting some init. cons. Has the tendency to add extra letters in words. Using some sight words. (is, it, a) -ing. 10/20

ARMANDO: Needs to work on spacing. Finally wrote L–R. Wonderful illustrations—really tell the story. Loves to draw! 10/20

CARMEN: Story doesn't make sense. This often happens. She often writes down words and letter she already knows. Needs work on formatting letters. 10/20

JASMINE: Reverses <u>W</u> sound with <u>R</u>. She had difficulty continuing w/orig. story line. W/suppot she writes well. Model rereading so she can go back and add punct. 10/20

In addition to the lesson topics mentioned in the chapter, here are some of the other mini-lessons we teach:

MINI-LESSONS

- How to sound out a word (invented spelling)
- What is a vowel? All words have vowels
- What is a consonant?
- Hard C / Soft C
- Hard C words/ K words
- Soft C words/ S words
- Hard G/ Soft G
- Soft G words/ J words
- Blends: gr, bl, br
- Digraphs: sh, th, ch, ph
- Long and short vowels
- Plurals
- Possessives
- Contractions
- Qu rule
- Suffixes: ing, ed, est, able, ible, ly
- double consonants:
  - change y to i
  - drop last e
- Prefixes: ex, dis, mis, re
- Silent letters: knife, whole, gnash
- Y as a consonant, y as a vowel i
- Different ways to spell the long and short i sound: idea, night, bite, try

- Different ways to spell the long e sound: be, feet, fear, he, receive, people, many, money
- Different ways to spell the short and long a sound: fair, wear, bare, weigh, day, they
- Different ways to spell the long o sound: bone, know, dough, no, toe
- Different ways to spell the u sound: you, pure, view, few
- Different ways to spell the sh sound: ship, nation, racial, sugar
- Homophones
- Antonyms
- Synonyms
- Where to get help with a spelling word:
  - a Word Wall
  - environmental print
  - personal word book
  - dictionary
  - peer/teacher help
- How to look up a word in a dictionary
- How to edit your writing for spelling

Patsy uses the grid format to make notes.

Aaron	**Alex**	**Alicia**	**Ashley**	**Asia**	**Bill**
	Work on spacing	-ed endings for past tense	Sh sounds Ch sounds	Rereading to see if marks make sense	
Calvin	**Chris**	**Edwin**	**Isaiah**	**Jasmin**	**Jason**
Needs to extend stories	Checking for spelling	New topic	Capitalization for names; beginning sentences		Uppercase I; Work on spacing
Jeffrey	**Jose**	**Keisha**	**Kiki**	**Roberto**	**Ricardo**
Capitalization of Cities and States	Spacing—remind to use fingers		Good speller; reread for meaning	Spacing	Encourage to use word book; ask for spelling
Ruth	**Samatha**	**Shawn**	**Simon**	**Stephanie**	**Taina**
Needs: They're Their There		Sh sounds	Neatness & spacing; uses only words he knows	Use of punctuation instead of and; period	Neatness
Teresa	**Victoria**	**Wendy**	**Winston**	**Zachary**	
	-ing endings -ed endings	Work on spacing		Needs: wasn't won't	

Creating a Spelling Program to Meet Individual Needs

Direct Teaching

In other sections of this book, we discuss the importance of setting up a language-rich classroom environment, in which we make it clear we value each child's ability to learn. This is important. However, just because our room is filled with print—from experience charts to stories and poems—there is no guarantee that children will learn to spell.

There are times when we teachers need to do direct teaching of spelling skills and strategies; that is, when we teach our children specific rules or patterns, such as blends, conventional spelling rules (*i* before *e* except after *c),* word families (*cat, fat, sat, mat*), and word endings (*ing* or *ed*). How do we decide when to teach these? We observe our children throughout the day, look at past assessment notes for these children, and conclude that a child or group of children needs help in that area.

For example, when Min realized that five children needed help with basic "sight words," she gathered these children in a group and read aloud *My Messy Room* by Mary Packard, a story which contains many basic words. (The children followed along in their own copies of the book.) The next day, she gathered the same children again and had them play word bingo to reinforce the words learned earlier. (See Chapter 2 for other useful spelling games.) We like to teach direct lessons like these at individual conferences, with small groups, or the whole class.

Individualized Spelling to Meet Children's Specific Needs

Each of us has our own strategies for teaching spelling. Below, we describe our strategies, indicating in parentheses which teacher is speaking.

Weekly Spelling List (Min)

I ask each child to create a weekly, individualized spelling list that consists of words the child wants to learn how to spell. Usually, the words come from the children's independent reading or writing. Children know that the purpose of the list is to help them learn how to spell specific words.

How does the system work? In the writing center, I set out a basket which contains blank weekly spelling lists. Children pick up a sheet at the beginning of the week and keep it in their folders. Any time they have difficulty spelling a word, they write it on the "Have a Go" (first try) section. For example: Keisha wrote a story about going to the school yard. Here is an example of Keisha's weekly spelling list. Though Keisha rarely needed any help with sight words, the three words she needed to learn to spell were important words to her story.

Keisha uses the "Have a Go" section to try and spell three words she uses in her story.

Sometimes, I suggest that children look at certain words more carefully. For example, first grader Tony was having a difficult time recognizing the vowels; he would use only beginning and ending consonants. His individualized spelling program focused on vowel sounds.

Tony's weekly spelling sheet shows he often doesn't use vowels.

The children work with their list for a few days, then take it home and review it with a parent or older sibling. Then they choose an in-class buddy (or I choose one for them) to see how well they have practiced their words.

The number of words on the weekly lists varies: Some children may have three words, while others may have more than five. At the end of the week, I check to see if there are words the child is still having trouble with and give him/her the option of putting those on the next week's spelling list.

I also use the spelling list at reading time. For example, during my guided reading lesson with one group, we came to the word *mosquito*. The children had a difficult time recognizing the word. When they used different clues to figure it out, they were surprised by its spelling.

Clues to Use

We encourage our children to use different clues to figure out how to read, write, or spell words. Often, the children themselves will come up with effective strategies, and we then make a point of celebrating this. For example, we might say, "Jennie, you just did something very interesting. You used the picture and then looked at the first letter and figured out what the word was!"

At the end of the guided reading lesson, I asked the children to write the word *mosquito*. When I looked at their spelling, nearly every child in the group had a unique way to spell it. (Without the book in front of them, they relied on their own skills to spell it.)

Armando:	mosquetitoe
Jasmine:	masqeto
Raymond:	makeydow
Jennifer:	masktow
Lisa:	mseo
Miguel:	moseto

When I asked them to look in the book for the actual spelling, Jasmine commented: "I should have known there would be a *q* and a *u* next to each other." She went on to say that when there is a *q*, a *u* always follows.

> ## READING CLUES
>
> ◆ Look at the picture.
>
> ◆ Skip the word, and see what word would make sense.
>
> ◆ Use an initial consonant with the picture.
>
> ◆ Break words into syllables.
>
> ◆ Think of other words that look similar (ex: say, day).

Personal Word Books (Patsy)

I give each child a personal word book, which is a small, spiral-bound notebook to which I've added tabs from A to Z (3–4 pages per letter, though you may want to devote more pages to *s* and *t* words and fewer to *z* words). These books hold a collection of words that the children need for their writing. We also add words at individual conferences.

I encourage children to ask for the conventional spellings of up to three new words a day, and the words are recorded in the book by me or another teacher. At first, children need reminders to use the word books, but soon the books become part of children's everyday tools.

Children like to add words to their word books from a friend's personal word book, and we gently point out that only correctly spelled words may be added. We're pleased that, over time, children build up word banks that they can use for future writing.

The word books are kept in the children's work cubbies and are used throughout the day, whenever children are writing. Children also find the books useful when editing their work.

Weekly Spelling List (Patsy)

I have created an individualized weekly spelling program, as I believe that assigning one spelling list to the whole class simply doesn't work. Children's range in ability is too great for such a "one-size-fits-all" approach. Therefore, once children are comfortable sounding out a lot of words, and are willing to take risks with new words, I begin the individualized spelling program. I wait a few weeks because I believe that if I begin too early, the child will become too focused on getting the conventional spelling, and this will interfere with the flow of writing.

Each day, I meet with five different children and work with each one individually. I choose a word from his or her writing or personal word book that the child frequently misspells. I show the child other words that follow the same pattern of spelling; for example, *night, fight, sight, fright.* I write these words on an index card for the child to take home and learn.

On the same day the next week, I meet with the child again and check if he/she has learned the words. If the child hasn't learned the words, or has not quite mastered them, I assign the same words for the following week. I only assign words appropriate for the child's level, so if a child writes:

Mi mom gve me a btfl nu drs.

My mom gave me a beautiful new dress.

I focus on *my* or *new* before the more difficult words like *beautiful.* So, the child's weekly spelling words might be:

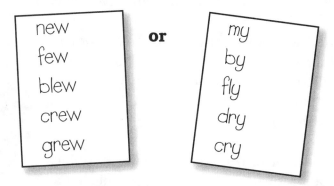

Since the spelling conference is the same day each week, children know when it is and to prepare for it. They help each other learn their words.

Word Wall (Min)

A Word Wall is an interactive list of words displayed on a wall chart. The words that are listed there are those generated by the children during writing conferences. Children use the chart throughout the day.

During a writing conference, I ask a child to pick a word to put on the Word Wall. I encourage the child to choose words other children might need to learn to spell, too. I also ask the child to choose words he/she

has spelled correctly or words spelled very close to the correct spelling.
For example, Bob wrote the following story:

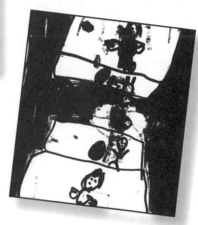

Yesterday
I plaed
soccr with
my brdr.

Yesterday I played
soccer with my brother.

In early writing, one sentence is often considered a story by a child.

Bob drew this picture to accompany his story.

Bob chose the word *yesterday* for the Word Wall. Bob and I also decided to put up the word *plaed*. When writing time was over, Bob shared his story with the class. Bob ended his sharing time by informing the children about the two new words (*yesterday* and *played*) that he had added to the Word Wall.

A "trade secret" that makes using the Word Wall much easier for children: Have them write the words they are adding to the Wall on strips of Post-it® Correction & Cover-up Tape. This allows children to remove a word from the Wall and bring it to their desks for reference when they're writing and want the correct spelling. (In the past, I had children write new words onto the actual Word Wall paper. In order to copy the spelling of a word, some children walked back and forth, from the wall to their desks, until they had copied each letter. This

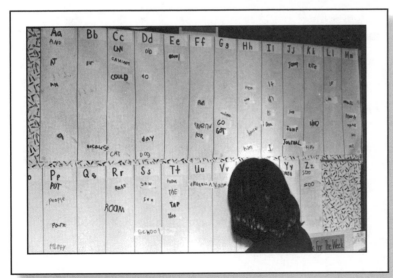

sometimes took as much as five minutes per word!) Eventually, we delete some words from the Word Wall, because children know how to spell them, thus making room for new words. For example, the words *the* and *and* became sight words, and we took them down.

Small Group Lessons

At times, we identify a group of children who need help in a specific area. (This group changes as the needs of individual children change.) Then we use one or more of the following strategies to teach the concept.

Lesson Extensions (Min)

After a lesson, I encourage children to meet as pairs to reread books or poems we have read as a class. They try to see how many word families they can find. For example, two children were rereading the poem "Mistress Pratt" by Arnold Lobel. They discovered *at* endings throughout the poem. They then decided to write on sticky notes other words ending in *at*, and added these words to a corner of the Word Wall.

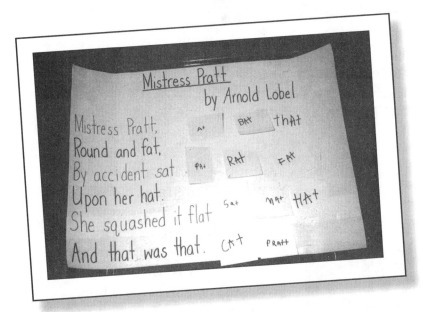

Two children read and reread the poem "Mistress Pratt" by Arnold Lobel, looking for word families. They then brainstormed a list of new at words.

Another example: As Dan and Raymond were reading the big book *The Hungry Giant* by Joy Cowley, they discovered the word *knocker*. We had been learning about *silent k* words in earlier lessons. Dan and Raymond realized that *knocker* was a word with a silent *k*, because they could only hear the letter *n*. They decided to make their own list of *kn* words. Examples: *knew / knot / knicks.*

Raymond helps Dan write kn *words on the list.*

Flip Books (Patsy and Min)

Using flip books, our students practice reading and spelling word families. We make flip books from sentence strips—one long piece at the bottom and five or six shorter pieces stapled together at the top left side. The long piece contains the root of the word (*ing*), and the short pieces (the flaps) have the initial letters (*r, s, th*). Children flip through the pack, reading aloud words such as *ring, sing, thing.* Another example: If the flip book has the root *at*, the first flap might have *b*, the next *c*, and so on to *th* and *br*. As the child turns each flap, he/she says the new word: *bat, cat, that, brat.*

After we work on a word family, children bring the flip books home to practice there. They soon build up a collection of flip books with various word families to practice at home.

We also make flip books for words that begin with the same sound, such as *sh* words. The letters *sh* are written on the long strip, which we place on the bottom, while word endings are written on the shorter pieces, which we place on top. Then we staple the book on the right.

| sh | ow | op | ip | ut | am | sh | ow |

Making flip books is a good follow-up activity for a mini-lesson on word endings, blends, or word families. Sometimes children work in groups to make them, sometimes they make them individually.

Whole Group Lessons

Daily News Chart (Patsy)

At the beginning of the year, I begin a Daily News chart, and the class continues writing Daily News charts every day. This ritual provides an opportunity to teach important spelling conventions and strategies.

Katherine is rereading the Daily News chart.

Each day, a few children share their news, which I then write on a chart. The chart begins each day with "Today is...". Children learn to write the days of the week, the months of the year, and the date. They learn that days and months are capitalized. I encourage children to sound out words, and I praise them for their efforts. I bring to their attention upper- and lowercase letters, initial sounds, word endings, contractions, and so forth. Many words are repeated day after day and become part of the children's sight vocabulary. Children take risks sounding out new words and learn by the example of others.

Each day, I focus attention on one or two elements I have chosen from the chart. At first, I might highlight words that begin with *th*, later it might be words that end in *ight*—whatever I notice in their writing. For example, if a child shares the news "Last night my dad took me to MacDonald's, and then we bought a new reading light," I'd use it as a jumping-off point to talk about words that end in *ight*. If I see a lot of contractions on the chart, I talk about them. One reason I like this activity is that different children learn different things from the chart, depending on their individual levels.

Children constantly refer to the Daily News chart when they need a word for their writing. They often go back to a chart written earlier that month to find a word they remember we used then. Children also enjoy copying the news to bring home to read to their parents, and of course, they love pointing to the chart and rereading it over and over again.

Personal Writing Shared With the Class (Min)

Throughout the year, I frequently model personal writing. I draft a story about myself on a dry-erase board, thinking aloud as I write. (Donald Graves calls this technique "reading the world.") Sometimes, I deliberately make spelling errors, then ask my children to correct my work (Q: "What's wrong with the way I spelled my name?" A: "It has a lowercase *h*!") The children see that writers edit their work, making changes to improve the way they communicate with readers.

My modeling—and the children's involvement in "assisting" me—helps them to become better risk takers during their own personal writing. I emphasize many of the same strategies and skills covered in Daily News chart lessons.

Kaye, a first-grade student, makes spelling corrections on a story written by the teacher.

Some months into the school year, I extend the personal writing lesson by asking a child for permission to use her/his personal writing with the class. If the child agrees, I invite that child to write a story on the board. Often, there are mistakes. For example, punctuation marks may be missing or upper- and lowercase letters used incorrectly.

So we edit the piece, using feedback from the rest of the group. "Why do you think it's hard to read this sentence?" I might ask. "Because there's no spacing after words. The words are mushed together," children respond. On another occasion, I might say, "What do you notice about *mary* and *john*'s names in this story?" The children will respond, "The *m* and *j* needs to be uppercase because it's someone's name."

The children take great pride in their work, especially when it is used as a teaching tool.

Strategies to Spell Difficult Words (Patsy)

Each year before I begin my individualized spelling program, I choose a difficult word like *treacherous* from a book that we're reading. By showing children that they can learn to spell a *long* word, I believe I give them confidence to learn to spell *any* word. We talk about what the word means, and, as a whole class, learn to spell it. Of course, I model strategies for learning to spell a word.

EXAMPLE

◆ Look at the word, and spell it out loud a few times.
   t-r-e-a-c-h-e-r-o-u-s
◆ Try to visualize it and spell it without looking.
   trchrus
◆ Break the word into syllables, and spell it.
   trech-er-us
◆ Write it down, and check back to see if it is correct.
   treacherus
◆ Repeat this process until you learn the word.
   treacherous

Children take turns trying to spell the word, and they help each other until everyone in the class knows how.

For the next few weeks, we ask everyone who enters our room, "Do you think we can spell the word *treacherous*?" Of course, everyone says, "No way!" Then my children gleefully spell *treacherous*. They go home and ask their families the same question (some placing bets before demonstrating their proficiency). Using the word *treacherous*, we play Scrambled Eggs (see next section), a game that shows children they can create smaller words using the letters in the larger word. For example, from *treacherous* they can find letters to spell *teacher, teach, our,* and *reach.*

Spelling Games and Activities

Games, such as letter races and crossword puzzles, are a fun way to reinforce skills learned at other times during the school day. Games can be played as a whole group, as a small group, or individually. We introduce games throughout the year, based on what the children need, or modify them to meet the children's ever-changing levels. For example, we intro-

duce letter races early in the year but wait until later in the year to introduce crossword puzzles. (That's because letter races, consisting of only
two columns, are relatively simple to play, while crossword puzzles
involve knowledge of the alphabet, of conventional spelling, and other
skills.) But no matter what the games are or their level of complexity,
children find them fun and learn from them at the same time. Here are a
few games we play.

Letter Races

Children love this game, which can be played with a large or small group.
Two letters "race" against each other as the children come up with as
many words as possible that begin with each letter. The letter with the
most words wins the race.

We start by creating two columns on a chart, and place a letter in each
column, such as *c* and *k*. We ask children to suggest words that belong in
each column. As children call out words, I write them in the appropriate
column. Children who predicted which letter would win get to see how
their predictions turned out.

At the beginning of the year, we hold letter races with initial letter sounds
only. As the year progresses, we use blends (*br*), digraphs (*ph, sh*), and
word endings (*ed, ing*). This is particularly effective for teaching children
the differences between hard C and soft C, and hard G and soft G. The
children begin to see a pattern for each set of words (for example, all the
hard C words have *a* or *o* or *u* after the *c*). We also use letter races for
teaching the differences between *sh* and *ch* words.

*First graders play
the letter race game
as a whole group.
Letters* c *and* k *are
emphasized.*

A good extension of this game is to have children look in books for words
containing the given sounds. For example, while reading, children use
sticky notes to write any words they find that have the *ch* sound.

Word Bingo

Played like regular bingo, word bingo is a favorite in our classrooms. Here's how we prepare the game.

We type a master list of high-frequency words into a computer, print it out, cut out each word, laminate them, and put the slips into a plastic bag. (See Appendix page 79 for the list.)

Then we make individual cards for the children by taking a 12-by-15-inch card and sectioning it off—five words down and three words across. We then type randomly any 15 words from our master list. We make many different cards (changing the words and their order). We give each child one card. (Laminated cards last longer.)

The caller has a large board with all the words on it and the bag of word cards. The caller picks one card from a basket, says the word, spells the word, and shows the card to the players. The caller then places the card on the appropriate space on the large board. (The caller places the card over the original word.) The players place markers on the words that are on their cards. At first, the children place the cards by matching the letters, but soon the words become part of the children's sight vocabulary. We ask the children to see who can be the first to cover the whole board, but the game continues until everyone has covered all their words.

Second graders play word bingo.

Crossword Puzzles

Crossword puzzles are a great way to encourage children to use a dictionary to check spelling. At first, we create crossword puzzles with picture clues (see illustration below).

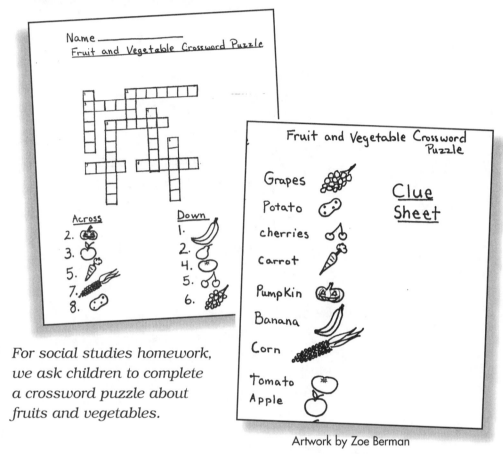

For social studies homework, we ask children to complete a crossword puzzle about fruits and vegetables.

Artwork by Zoe Berman

As children gain more experience, we use puzzles with word clues. Children also enjoy making their own puzzles for friends to solve. Children work in pairs or small groups to solve the puzzles. This is a good activity because children need to know the conventional spelling to find words. Sometimes, children use a dictionary to see if that's actually how the word is spelled.

Sometimes we use crosswords related to class themes. In the puzzle shown above, our theme was "How Fruits and Vegetables Come to New York City." That's why words such as *pumpkin* or *cherries* appear there. Rather than construct puzzles on our own, we sometimes use computer software such as *Spell It Deluxe or Morphabet Soup* (Davidson). In a word search, children look on a grid for words spelled horizontally, vertically, and diagonally.

Name_____

 Mix-Up Files Word Search

```
A M E R I C A N W I N G E L V T U K S M
R E J O P D S T C L V A J D E N P T U O
P D C N K R L S N A C X S N O Y L B E G
F I B S D O T Q J M V O K L T S J C A O
C E R T M A R M S A N D A R M O R D V X
T V S N C D B S U L T E C J K R N B O S
J A S M O V B L I K D E M O B P J K U
N L P B S J Q U E B E G R E A T H A L L
S A F T U N O B A R J O T U M O E P K N
P R K T E C U J K A B M O J Q R J M L E
E T M N O D E L D R C T M N E L V T J K
B L V J P K V E G Y P T I A N A R T O E
G R E E K A N D R O M A N A R T E B L P
```

The *Great Hall*, *Egyptian Art*, *Greek and Roman Art*, *Arms and Armor*, *Medieval Art*, the *American Wing* and the *Library* are all sections of The Metropolitan Museum of Art. Find them in this puzzle, and then we'll find them in the museum!

After enjoying a read-aloud of The Mixed-Up Files of Mrs. Basil E. Frankwelier, *children search for words on a puzzle made by student teacher Carrie Klein.*

Word-Search Puzzles

Word searches are a great homework activity because parents can easily participate and offer guidance. Sometimes as a follow-up to a mini-lesson taught in class, we place words in the word-search puzzle from a word family *(can, man, ran)*. Other times, we use words from a curriculum theme, such as transportation or community workers.

We also invite children to create word-search puzzles for their friends to solve, and remind them to use a dictionary to check the spelling before creating their puzzles. At first, we teach children how to write words vertically and horizontally. Once children get the idea, they begin to write words diagonally, as well. To create their word searches, we give children graph paper with large squares.

Wordswithinwords (Min)

This is a game the children and I play after writing a story on the board. For example, one day I wrote this story about my mother's birthday. (We were working on the use of punctuation marks and uppercase letters.)

yesterday was my mothers birthday
I baked her a chocolate cake it was
yummy I wonder if she had fun

First we made all the changes needed in the story. When the children finished adding and editing, the story looked like this:

Yesterday was my mother's birthday.
I baked her a chocolate cake. It was
yummy. I wonder if she had fun?

I asked the children to look for words within words. The children came up with this:

Yesterday was my mother's birthday.
I baked her a chocolate cake. It was
yummy. I wonder if she had fun?

I left the story on the board for the rest of the day so they could keep looking for more words. By the end of the day, there was a huge mess on the board, filled with new words they had found in other words. This is how it looked:

Yesterday was my mother's birthday.
I baked her a chocolate cake. It was
yummy. I wonder if she had fun?

Leaving the story displayed for the children helped them to continue searching for even more words. Children thought they had found every word possible, until Shawn shouted, "I found another one!" Shawn went to the board and squared off the word *birth* in the word *birthday.* I was surprised that Shawn had discovered another word, considering the mess we had made. This game really showed how many words the children knew how to spell.

Scrambled Eggs

This game has probably been called by many names. A colleague calls it Scrambled Eggs. We usually choose a word related to our social studies theme and ask the children—as a whole class or in small groups—to unscramble the letters to find as many smaller words as possible.

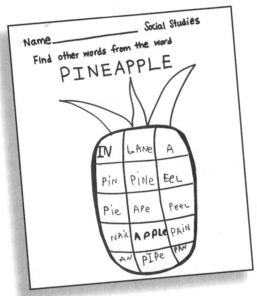

For social studies homework, children unscrambled the word pineapple *to find other words.*

We have also assigned this game as homework. Parents have commented that it is a fun activity to do as a family.

As with the other games, we encourage children to use a dictionary or other resource to check to see if they have actually spelled a word correctly. For example, one group in Min's classroom was unscrambling the word *watermelon.* The children in that group came up with an amazing list of smaller words. But one word they struggled with was *wale.* (They were trying to spell *whale* so they could add it to the list.) Since they weren't sure if it was correct, and couldn't find it in the dictionary, they asked Min. "We think it's spelled like this: *w-a-l-e,*" they said. At that moment, Juana turned to the group and said, "Let's get the book *Amos and Boris* (by William Steig)." Juana remembered the word *whale* in the story. The group found the book in the class library, searched for the word, then let out a sigh. One said, "Oh, we can't use it because *whale* has an *h* and there's no *h* in *watermelon*."

Richie commented: "We should have known it was spelled like *what*, *where*, *when*. They all start with the *wh*." We're sure this experience will always help these children remember how *whale* is spelled.

The Missing L_tt_ _s

This game has some similarities to the game Hang Man. We prefer to call it The Missing Letters Game. Often, we model this activity during whole group writing time.

We write a story on the board, one that tells about something that happened in the classroom. We leave out some letters for some words. (For example, in the story below, we left out *ing* and *ed*.) Then, as a group, we read the story together, as if it's a choral reading. (Because of the story format, the children are able to guess the words from the context.) Then we read it a second time—slowly—this time asking the children to help us finish spelling the incomplete words. For example:

> This morn_ _ _ we receiv_ _ a
> package from California. We had a
> hard time open_ _ _ the package.
> When we finally open _ _ it, there
> were 26 peanut butter cups.

> This morn<u>i</u> <u>n</u> <u>g</u> we receiv<u>e</u> <u>d</u> a
> package from California. We had a
> hard time open<u>i</u> <u>n</u> <u>g</u> the package.
> When we finally open <u>e</u> <u>d</u> it, there
> were 26 peanut butter cups.

If you do the missing letters activity with your class, you may want to start with stories, but, after a while, you may want to place isolated words on the board. You can even use words from social studies, science, or other subjects.

Mystery Words

During shared reading time, we pause in our reading aloud of a big book and cover up a word. Then we ask the children, "What word do you think is covered under the Post-it®?" The children make guesses by using picture clues, by rereading, and by reading ahead for meaning. If a child guesses the word *hungry*, we read the word, using it in the sentence. If the sentence makes sense, we uncover the first letter, asking the children, "What do you think? Do you think the word is still *hungry*? How do you think the word *hungry* is written?" The children make guesses. We start to uncover each letter of the word or chunks of letters.

Many children think the last letter in the word *hungry* might be an *e*. Often, the children have been surprised to see a *y*. They begin to realize that certain words may sound like they end with *e* but see that they end with a *y*; for example: *hungry, carry, lady, candy, friendly.* This activity develops children's awareness that words may sound alike but be spelled differently.

Chapter 4

A Look at Children's Spelling Over Two Years

The Spelling Progress of Four Students

We are fortunate to be working in the same school. It has given us an opportunity to analyze our spelling program closely by looking at our children's work over a two-year period.

We decided to study the spelling progress of four of our students. (We selected four whose spelling levels varied.) We examined each child's past and present work to assess development. Most importantly, we looked for each child's strength and areas in which each child struggled as a speller. In fact, it was this investigation that led us to see how crucial it is to tailor a spelling program to meet the needs of each child.

Let's look at how four children—Keisha, Kiki, Ricardo, and Bill—developed over time.

Keisha in First Grade

Keisha—a girl from a Spanish-speaking home—entered first grade with great enthusiasm, wanting to learn how to read and write. She was a risk taker and nothing, or no one, would stand in the way of her writing stories or pretending to read the words in books.

Keisha used the first few minutes of writing workshop to think about stories she wanted to write, then she'd draw a picture about the story. In her writing, she often experimented with letters, sometimes including words she already knew how to write, such as *Mom*. In fact, this word appeared in many of her stories, even if the story had nothing to do with her mom.

By looking at her illustrations, Keisha was always able to reread her stories to me or her peers. The stories that she told were elaborate and very detailed for a six-year-old. Within a few months, Keisha became a prolific writer, using initial consonants, environmental print, and lots of sight words (*are, is, the, and, it, was, that*). By the middle of June, Keisha wrote with great confidence, using many sight words, but she relied heavily on invented spelling. She still left out punctuation marks, spaces, and was uncomfortable with using upper- and lowercase letters in her work. To help, I gave her the writing rubric the children and I had developed together. Written in the children's words, it outlined ways to self-edit our work (see Appendix, page 80). I pointed out these details when we met in a conference.

Keisha's First-Grade Writing Samples

We got a pumpkin. I like the pumpkin.

I will be a dentist and a teacher and a lion trainer when I grow up.

Keisha in Second Grade

In second grade, Keisha still loves to write and does so with a great deal of imagination. In September, she wrote a few sentences each day, accompanied by a detailed picture. She rarely used punctuation and had not mastered the correct use of uppercase letters. Keisha's writing was still difficult to decipher because of a lack of spacing. She was aware of that and knew how to space her writing, but she wrote fast and was reluctant to pay attention to that element of her work. (When Keisha writes for publication, she uses spacing correctly.)

How did I address Keisha's problems? In addition to giving her time and immersing her further in writing, I asked her to self-edit her work. For example, I might say, "Keisha, before putting away your work, do you think you can reread it and see if there are places you need to go over?" In addition, Keisha used a conference checklist (see Appendix) to edit her work.

By the fourth month of second grade, Keisha's spelling is much closer to conventional spelling, and she has a large sight vocabulary. In addition, she takes risks with sounding out more words. Keisha doesn't always use her personal word book and has to be reminded to ask for three words a day. Keisha is beginning to use contractions correctly in her writing. She still has some letter reversals but, when asked to, can reread and correct them. Keisha needs help with words with the *oa* sound in the middle, such as *boat, goat, cloak,* and *throat,* and words with the *ight* ending, such as *might, night, sight.*

Keisha's Second-Grade Writing Samples

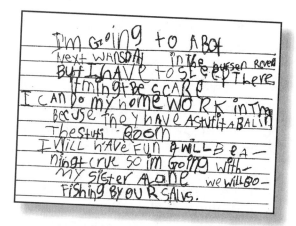

Last week my brother came to visit me and my sister. We had a party. His name is John.

I'm going to a boat next Wednesday in the Hudson River. But I have to sleep there. I might be scared. I can do my homework in there because they have a study table in the study room. I will have fun. It will be a night cruise so I am going with my sister alone. We will go fishing by ourselves.

KIKI

Kiki in First Grade

Kiki came into first grade as an independent reader and a prolific writer. She's from a Chinese-speaking home. By the time she entered my class, she had memorized many sight words and written many words using conventional spelling.

In the beginning of the year, Kiki often wrote stories about herself and her family or things that happened in school. Somehow, she got the idea that good writing is synonymous with lots of words on a page, so she often wrote stories with the goal of trying to reach the bottom of the paper.

When we'd meet for a conference, we'd most often work on spacing, punctuation marks, and sequencing of events. Teaching Kiki to reread her stories helped her learn to go back and self-edit. She learned to slow down and put spaces in between words. When rereading her stories, she began to place punctuation marks in the right places.

Kiki rarely had difficulty spelling words. Often, she wrote the correct letters, but they appeared in the wrong order, for example, *slied* for *slide*. Showing her the rules of *silent e* helped her to spell *slide* as well as other words (such as *hide, side, wide*). Introducing spelling rules (*qu, ed*) and word families helped her, too. The wonderful thing about Kiki is that these spelling glitches didn't stand in the way of her writing. She was a risk taker, and she began to explore different genres as a writer.

Kiki's First-Grade Writing Samples

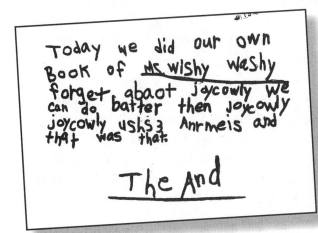

Today we did our own book of *Mrs. Wishy Washy*. Forget about Joy Cowley. We can do better than Joy Cowley. Joy Cowley uses 3 animals and that was that.

This is a story about saff
I ramber And a make-up story

One ce there was a bird and cow
they always fight for worms then
One day a squirrel comes simm
ing in the water they could ed
belivile that a squirrel can simm
in water they were sapise.

THE END!!!!!!!

This is a story about stuff I remember and a make up story. Once there was a bird and crocodile. They always fight for worms. Then one day a squirrel came swimming in the water. They couldn't believe that a squirrel can swim in water. They were surprised.

Second Grade

In second grade, Kiki continues to be a prolific writer who experiments with different genres. She enjoys writing and often chooses to do so during free time. Kiki is also an avid reader, and various literary influences can be seen in her writing.

At the beginning of second grade, Kiki would often write a few sentences, accompanied by a picture. While her spelling was almost all conventional, she still put letters in the wrong order in words, for example, *geart* for *great*. Kiki was beginning to grasp many of the conventions of punctuation, such as periods, but was not always using exclamation points and commas correctly. Kiki also needed help with the use of uppercase *I* for first person and the correct use of upper- and lowercase letters.

By the fourth month of second grade, Kiki has mastered many more conventions. She writes pages each day and loves to share her work. Reading with great expression, she's even started to use dialogue in her stories and is mastering the use of quotation marks. Kiki's use of punctuation, such as question marks, exclamation points, and apostrophes, shows an understanding of their use, but she needs more instruction in the use of commas. I will work with her on this.

Now Kiki is more consistent in the correct use of upper- and lowercase letters, as shown by her use of uppercase letters for names, beginnings of sentences, and for *I*. She also uses contractions and possessives correctly. Kiki is working on rereading her work for self-editing and does a good job, using her spelling book or a dictionary to check words she isn't sure about. Kiki is learning the rules for doubling a consonant before adding a suffix (for example: *run–running*) and the use of plurals.

Kiki's Second-Grade Writing Samples

Today is the third
day of School.

And i am already
excited.about
second grade! Becau
se, i am wondering

What i am going
to learn in second
grade! The end!

Today is the third day of
school. And I am already
excited about second grade
because I am wondering
what I am going to learn in
second grade.

Once upon a time, There lived a
girl named Mary ann. She had red
rosed cheeks. And beautiful brownish
hair She lived in a very emty house.
But She was caughat one day, And
a stranger killed her. And in return
the house became haunted It got dark
and dirty in the house And furnentures
where knocked down. And one day as
a young girl came skiping along, She
spotted the chair get knocked down,
And decided to go on in and take a look
But she decide, to ask her mother
to go and take a look instead. But
fist she wanted to go and exsplore
the place by herslef, But she was
a little scared. So she decided to go
with har friends to exsplore. So after
the ghost of Mary ann had stoped knocking
Next page

down stuff cause she saw the little
girl she thought about her little child.
So now she decided to go and find her
little child So she flew out the window and
off she went to look for her child. She
flew and flew to the park. And found
her child with her friends. She wisepered
in her wispery voice "Angleina Angleina"
And when Angkina (the little girl) heard
someone calling her. She remembered her mothers
voice. She ran and followed the voice until
it got quiet. So the little girl saw her
mom and she cried "Mommy!" .!
She quickily tarned away.

RICARDO

Ricardo in First Grade

Ricardo entered his first-grade classroom in the middle of December. He had no prior schooling. He was put into first grade based on his age. Ricardo spent most of writing time drawing pictures of people. After about a month, he learned to write his name. He was very proud that he was able to write his name on his work.

During the first year with Ricardo, we spent most of our time teaching him the alphabet, the formation of letters, and getting him to feel comfortable drawing his stories, rather than forcing him to write words. Ricardo's parents requested that I keep him in first grade for another year. I recommended that Ricardo get some extra help during the summer.

When September arrived, Ricardo was one of the first children to enter the classroom. He greeted me as if we'd never said good-bye. He seemed different. He showed more confidence, and I even overheard him telling another child, "I know where everything is in here." He was showing off to the other children that the classroom was a familiar place to him. I was relieved when I saw that Ricardo was comfortable to be in the same classroom again.

Ricardo still spent more time on illustrating than writing. However, he learned to use environmental print effectively. Sometimes, he just wrote strings of letters, and his name would appear somewhere in the story. Eventually, he knew some sight words *(the, and, I'm, to)* and used invented spelling.

Ricardo had a difficult time spacing after every word. To help him in that area, I showed him how spacing is used in published books. Then I modeled for him by placing two fingers after each word to make a space. This was a major objective for Ricardo's writing, and I worked with him on it for the rest of the year.

Ricardo's First-Grade Writing Samples

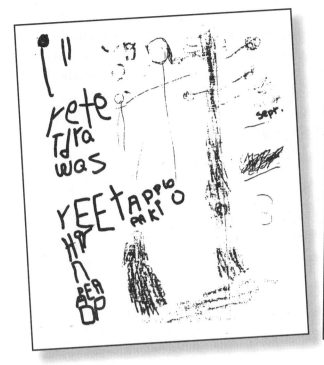

Yesterday I went apple picking.

I'm going to the Toy's 'Я' Us and I'm going to buy Spiderman figure.

Ricardo in Second Grade

It was a confident Ricardo who entered my second-grade classroom this year. He was eager to write and could often be heard offering help to other children in sounding out words. He was also one of the first to volunteer to share his writing with the class (though he often needed help rereading his work).

In September, Ricardo's writing consisted of almost all invented spelling (beginning and ending consonants with a vowel in the middle) with very few sight words. He was beginning to space his words, though he didn't always write from the top to the bottom of the page. I noticed that Ricardo had difficulty identifying the difference between words that start with the same letter but end differently, such as *dust* and *different*. A colleague visiting the room suggested outlining each word so he could see the shape of the word (see sample on next page). This has helped. Four months into second grade, Ricardo has developed a large sight vocabulary and has close to conventional spelling with many other words.

Ricardo is beginning to use periods at the end of sentences, though he is not always consistent. He still uses uppercase letters in the middle of sentences, and while this is something we talk about, it is not something I choose to dwell on since it might interfere with the flow of his writing. I do focus on word families, though, such as *ill* words *(hill, will, till)* to point out patterns that will help him in the future. I also remind Ricardo to use his personal spelling book more frequently to support him while writing.

Ricardo's Second-Grade Writing Sample

This week I went to Barnes and Noble with my cousin. I read 30 books.

BILL

Bill in First Grade

Bill entered first grade with some sight words and used initial consonants to sound out words. However, he was so worried about knowing the "correct" spelling that he only wrote stories with words he already knew how to spell. When Bill and I conferenced together, he would relate other stories that were more creative. For a long time, Bill consistently wrote stories describing someone or something. For example, many of his stories began with the words *this* or *the*:

"This is me." "This is my shoes." "This is my mom." "The dog is happe."

To help Bill overcome his fear of writing, I showed him how close he was to conventional spelling. For example:

hapstr (**ham**st**er**)   see (**sea**)   dantist (**de**ntist)

This gave him more confidence, and by June, Bill was writing stories that related to him personally. He used punctuation marks appropriately and used conventional spelling. However, he still hesitated in writing longer stories.

Bill's First-Grade Writing Samples

This is my house. I have a pet. It is a hamster.

The kid went to the dentist because he eats too much junk food and he got a cavity.

Bill in Second Grade

In second grade, Bill still avoids taking risks. He often writes as little as possible, rarely extending himself. With encouragement, Bill is beginning to write more. He has mastered many of the conventions of writing and can read over and edit his own work, especially with the use of his spelling book and a dictionary. I encourage Bill to extend his writing and to choose new topics and genres. He is also learning the correct use of capitalization.

He is inclined to incorrectly use uppercase *b* (probably because his name begins with a *B*). Bill can reread his work to correct this, which tells me he knows the correct usage. He has not quite internalized the use of uppercase *I* when talking about himself, but can go back and correct it if asked to do so. When Bill learns his new spelling words, he usually uses them correctly in his writing. Because Bill is a fluent reader, he realizes when words are not "book" spelling. I also notice words that we have not worked on become sight words for him, probably because he reads them so often. Many of Bill's misspelled words are close to conventional spelling. He often misses only one letter (*broght* for *brought*, *anather* for *another*) or places letters in an incorrect position (*houes* for *house*). Bill has mastered the correct use of periods and is consistent in their use. My plan is to brainstorm with him words that contain the vowel combinations *ie* and *oa*, such as *field, shield, yield* and *goal, foal, boat, goat*.

Bill's Second-Grade Writing Samples

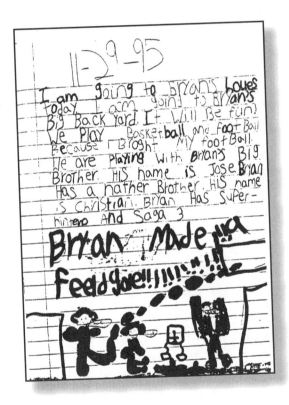

I am going to Bryan's house today. I am going to Bryan's big backyard. It will be fun! We play basketball and football because I brought my football. We are playing with Bryan's big brother. His name is Jose. Bryan has another brother. His name is Christian. Bryan has Super Nintendo and Sega 3. Bryan made a field goal!

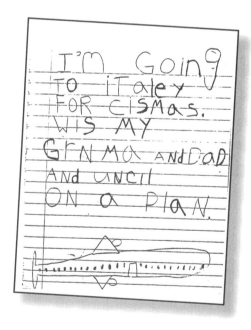

I'm going to Italy for Christmas. With my grandma and dad and uncle on a plane.

Chapter 5

Evaluation and Assessment

A Mirror on Our Teaching

Assessment is an ongoing process in our classrooms. We use assessment to gauge each individual child's growth and needs, and to inform us about our teaching.

By looking at the accumulation of children's work, we can assess what strategies have worked well and what we need to revise. We can also see which children have grasped certain concepts and who needs additional help. We sometimes find that we have to search for other ways to teach a concept to meet the learning styles of *all* our children.

For us, assessment takes place in formal and informal ways. Here are some examples from our classrooms:

FORMAL ASSESSMENT

Conferences

Though this book is on spelling, it is hard to isolate spelling from the writing process. Since we teach spelling in context, our conferences with children include all areas of editing, not just spelling.

We hold conferences with each child about once a week. A conference may take anywhere from five to fifteen minutes per child. A first conference will focus on writing issues, such as stating ideas sequentially. At a later conference, we'll concentrate on spelling alone.

Here is an example of how a writing conference might develop:

1. The child reads his/her piece to the teacher.
2. The teacher asks questions about the piece. ("What is the most important thing you are saying in your story?" "Which part is your favorite?")
3. The teacher asks the child if there is something he/she would like help with, such as writing an exciting title or explaining more clearly how to play a game.
4. The teacher then focuses on this area to help the child. This may or may not be spelling, as the teacher will work with the child on this piece again.
5. The child works on the piece again, editing the area focused on during conference time. (See next page for an example of a child's work.)
6. The child rereads the piece to the teacher before reading it to the class.

WORK SAMPLES

At a later date, before publishing the piece, the conference may focus on spelling alone.

1. **The child reads the piece to the teacher.**

   1. I sw John sd by the limzne.
   (I saw John stand by the limousine)

2. **The teacher asks the child to identify words with which he/she needs help.**

   2. s d, l m z n e
   (stand, limousine.)

3. **The teacher picks one word and asks the child to "have a go" (try again).**

   3. s t d

4. **The teacher indicates which letters are correct by putting a check over the correct letters.**

   4. s̆t̆d̆ (✓✓✓)

5. **The teacher asks the child to think of words that sound the same, look the same (word family) as the word.**

   5. h |and|

6. **The teacher asks which part of the new word will help him spell the word.**

   6. _ _ |and|

7. **The teacher helps the child put the pieces together to spell the word correctly.**

   7. s̲ t̲ |and|

8. **The word is added to the child's individual spelling book and/or to the Word Wall.**

   8. stand

WHAT TO LOOK FOR DURING A CONFERENCE

While conferring with children, we look at many aspects of spelling as well as other writing skills:

- left to right directionality
- top to bottom directionality
- spacing
- does writing match pictures
- does title match story
- using sight words
- using environmental print, Word Wall, etc.
- using spelling book
- capitalization
  - beginnings of sentences
  - names
  - use of I
- punctuation
  - periods
  - question marks
  - exclamation points
  - quotation marks
  - apostrophes
  - commas

- plurals
  - s
  - es
  - new endings
- possessives
- suffixes
  - ing
  - ed
  - er
- blends and digraphs
- silent letters
- sentence structure
- use of new words
- willingness to sound out words
- almost-conventional spelling
- compound words
- contractions
- editing for meaning

Min confers with Rosanna in preparation for publication.

Conference Notes

After each conference, we make notes. These are my (Min's) conference notes for Roselda:

10/13
Roselda needs work w/spacing. Has difficulty rereading story b/c of no spacing. Show a big book

10/26
Roselda doing better w/spacing. Still needs some reminding. Doing better w/spelling—taking more risks.

11/14
Roselda working on fairy tale. Finally! something different. Good job use of sight words. Great spacing.

12/06
Roselda—lovely stories. Moving slowly away from illust. Still not rereading. Model this for her.

1/08
Roselda—she's experimenting w/punct. marks. Rereading. is gaining a lot of sp. words. Mixing up U and l case letters.

1/21
Roselda doing well w/flow of writing (fluency). Rereading and self correcting words—great. Still has diff. w/lower case. Ex: One Boy Took a Jacket.

2/4
Roselda curious about Q & A. We decided to do a dialogue journal. Teach and model good questioning (research). Letters a and e. Practice.

Focus on Children's Needs

Once we've collected all the information about what children can and cannot do, we use that to inform our teaching. How is this done? We bring together small groups of children who have the same needs for a mini-lesson. If many children have the same need, we teach a whole group mini-lesson. We use notes on individual children to see growth over time and identify issues that need to be addressed at individual conferences.

Plurals			
dog	dogs	fox	foxes
doll	dolls	sandwich	sandwic
cat	cats	glass	glasse
boy	boys	box	boxes
ball	balls	bush	bushes
book	books	bus	buses
teacher	teachers	class	classes
movie	movies	flash	flashes
skate	skates	crash	crashes
sister	sisters	rash	rashes
gift	gifts	gross	grasses
balloon	balloons	ash	ashes
coat	coats	smash	smashes
building	buildings	branch	branches
house	houses	lunch	lunches

A plurals chart made with children at a whole group lesson.

PORTFOLIOS

Student's Portfolio Selection

Three times a year (in November, March, and June), we work with individual children, looking through all their work to help them choose one piece to add to their ongoing portfolios. We ask the child to choose a piece that shows his growth as a writer. The child uses a sticky note to write why he chose that piece. Children's comments include: "I like this piece because my spelling is like in books." and "This is good work because now I know the *ing* sounds."

Teacher's Portfolio Selection

On a regular basis, we look at the child's accumulation of work to assess his/her growth and areas of need. This is different from the example above because the child is not involved in the assessment.

Mahle, a first grader, sorts through his writing to choose one piece to add to his portfolio.

Patsy looks through a child's work for assessment before meeting with the child.

Children of this age often choose a piece for the portfolio because they like the topic or how the piece looks. We choose writing pieces to make sure that the child's portfolio reflects growth in *all* areas of writing, and we also document areas that the child needs help with. For example, if a child frequently misspells the word *were*, we note this.

INFORMAL ASSESSMENT

Ongoing Observation

We circulate around the room during writing time, glancing over the children's shoulders as they work, chatting with them about their progress. Often, we jot down our observations and the results of our informal dialogues. The following is a sample conversation:

Teacher: How's your writing going?

Child: How do you spell *winter*?

Teacher: Can you tell me two different ways you can try to spell this word?

Child: I'm not sure.

Teacher: Well, I'm looking at your piece, and I see you tried spelling the word *freezing* (*frezing*). How did you do that?

Child: I knew it started with *f*, and then I tried sounding it out, and then I remembered our *ing* list, so I knew it ended in *ing*.

Teacher: See how you used different strategies to spell just one word! Do you think you could try different ways with the word *winter*?

Sample Anecdotal Note:

> Applying knowledge of ing to figure out freezing.

Note Needed Strategies

Another way we assess our children is by observing their responses during lessons. For example, during a lesson, a child may use a strategy that shows she has grasped that convention or that she needs more help.

Then we take a minute after the lesson to jot down notes for that child. For example: While writing the Daily News, one child suggests *hom* for the word *home*. Since we have just worked on words that follow that pattern, we see that the child needs more help to master that spelling rule. We'll remind ourselves—in our notes—to follow up on it later.

Content Area Writing

We also look at children's writing in the content areas to see if they are applying the conventions they have learned. For example, when we look at a child's science observation, we might notice that the child has mastered the conventions of capitalization and spacing and has developed a larger sight vocabulary.

Troubleshooting

Naturally, we use many different occasions to assess areas where children need help, and we find time during the day to assist children or make plans to assist them in the future. Although we could have written an entire chapter on how we help children, we decided to focus on three important areas. These are:

- endings
- spacing
- plurals

Help with *ing* endings

If a small group of children has difficulty grasping the use of *ing*, we may help them by:

- making flip books of *ing* words.
- brainstorming a list of *ing* words.
- looking for *ing* words in newspapers and magazines.
- using a book with a lot of *ing* words for guided reading.
- playing games involving *ing* words.
- having children find *ing* words on charts around the room.

Spacing

If the whole class needs help with spacing, we:

- write a story on the board to show how difficult it is to read a piece with no spacing.
- write a sentence on a sentence strip, cut it up, and have children physically space the sentence.
- model, using fingers to put a space after each word.

Plurals

If an individual child has trouble with using correct plurals, we:

◆ show the child patterns that occur with plurals, such as *cups, shoes, friends* and *foxes, boxes, glasses.*

◆ have the child look for different plurals in books.

◆ have the child brainstorm plurals that fit a pattern.

Summing Up

While writing this book together, we were reminded how important it is for teachers to have dialogues with each other about children and about good teaching practices. Through our many conversations with each other, we have been able to share strategies that work and find effective ways to reach individual children.

We should mention that some months ago, we asked our colleagues, "What are some major obstacles in creating confident, creative, and prolific writers?" All the teachers mentioned spelling. Because of that response, we continue testing old strategies and finding new ones to make the teaching of spelling easier and more productive. We create an environment in class in which risk taking is a natural process, so that children overcome their fears about how words are spelled and write enthusiastically. Children's questions about writing change from "How do you spell _____?" to "Do you want to know what I did today as a writer?"

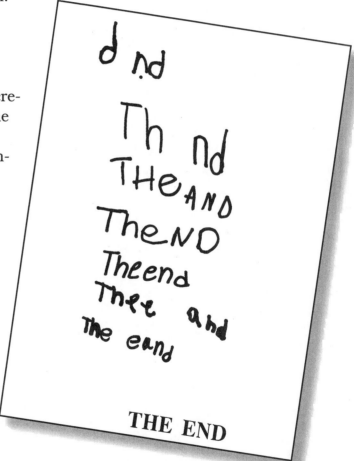

THE END

We hope this book will be a useful tool to help you get started teaching spelling successfully. In additon to what you already have read, we advise *you* to converse with and question yourselves, your students, and your colleagues. In fact, we suggested to our first graders that they give us advice on how to finish this book, and they said, "Write *The End*." So we did just that, using their own spellings of those words.

Appendix

A Guide to the Reproducibles

Sight Words/High-Frequency Words (page 69)

These are some basic words we'd like our children to learn to read. We use this list for word bingo games and weave them into Daily News writing as well as other writing experiences.

Letter Race (page 70)

We write a different letter at the bottom of each column (such as *c* and *k*), then conduct the race, as described in Chapter 3 of this book.

Teacher Conference Checklist (page 71)

Three times a year, we look through children's work, then complete this checklist.

First Grade Conference Checklist (page 73)

Children use this to help them self-edit their work.

Second Grade Conference Checklist (page 74)

(Same as 1st grade.)

Alphabet Letters (page 75)

Place this guide in children's writing folders to help them remember letter formation and punctuation marks.

Weekly Spelling List (page 76)

Any time children have difficulty spelling a word, they make a first attempt by writing it in the left-hand column. On the right, the teacher writes the conventional spelling.

Things I Can Do/Things I Need Help With (page 77)

Using this chart, a student looks through his work and makes a list of things he can do and what he needs help with.

About My Writing (page 78)

A self-evaluation sheet for children.

High-Frequency Words for Bingo (page 79)

Use these words to play word bingo.

Writing Rubric (page 80)

A writing rubric designed by Min and her first graders. The rubric looks at six criteria in writing. The rubric set standards for what a published piece should look like in first grade.

Sight Words/High-Frequency Words

about	every	know	one	they
after	family	last	only	thing
again	father	left	or	think
all	fell	let	other	this
also	find	like	our	through
always	first	little	out	time
am	for	live	over	to
an	friend	long	people	told
and	from	look	place	too
another	fun	lot	play	took
any	gave	love	put	two
are	get	mad	ran	under
around	girl	made	really	until
as	give	man	ride	up
ask	go	many	right	upon
at	going	may	run	us
back	good	me	said	very
be	dot	men	saw	walk
because	had	money	school	want
been	happy	more	see	was
before	has	most	she	way
best	have	mother	should	we
big	he	much	sister	well
boy	heard	my	small	went
brother	help	name	so	were
but	her	need	some	what
by	here	never	soon	when
called	him	new	started	where
came	his	next	take	which
can	home	nice	tell	who
come	house	night	ten	why
could	how	no	than	will
day	if	not	that	with
did	in	now	the	work
do	into	of	their	would
down	is	off	them	year
eat	it	old	then	yes
end	just	on	there	you
ever	knew	once	these	your

Letter Race

Teacher Conference Checklist

SKILL	DATE:	DATE:	DATE:
Left to right directionality			
Top to bottom directionality			
Spacing			
Does writing match pictures			
Does title match story			
Using sight words			
Uses environmental print, Word Wall, etc.			
Uses spelling book			
Capitalization: Beginning of sentence			
Names			
Use of "I"			
Punctuation: Periods			
Question marks			
Exclamation points			
Quotation marks			
Apostrophes			
Commas			

Teacher Conference Checklist (page 2)

SKILL	DATE:	DATE:	DATE:
Plurals: s			
es			
new endings			
Possessives			
Suffixes: ing			
ed			
er			
Blends and digraphs			
Silent letters			
Sentence structure			
Use of new words			
Willingness to take words			
Almost-conventional spelling			
Compound words			
Contractions			
Editing for meaning			

First Grade
Conference Checklist

Did you stamp the date?

Is there a title for your writing?

Did you draw pictures to go with your writing?

Is there a space between each word?

Did you dedicate your writing to someone?

Did you share your writing with someone?

Checker's Name:

Second Grade Conference Checklist

Child's Name _____

Date	
Title	
Author	
Illustrator	
Illustrations	
Dedication	
Spacing Between Words	
Periods at Ends of Sentences	
Uppercase *I*	
Uppercase Letters	
Beginning of Sentence	
Names	
Lowercase Letters	
Middle of Sentences	
Question Marks?	
Exclamation Points!	
"Quotation Marks"	
Endings ing, ed, s, es, er	
Meaning	
Spelling Using Dictionary	

Did you share your writing with someone?

Alphabet Letters

Aa	Bb	Cc	Dd	Ee
Ff	Gg	Hh	Ii	Jj
Kk	Ll	Mm	Nn	Oo
Pp	Qq	Rr	Ss	Tt
Uu	Vv	Ww	Xx	Yy
Zz	.	?	!	" "

Period.	Question Mark?	Exclamation Point!	"Quotation Marks"

Date _____

_____'s Weekly Spelling List

Have a Go . . .	Help From My Friend or Teacher . . .

I practiced with _____ at home.

I practiced with my friend _____ at school.

Name: _____

Things I Can Do	Things I Need Help With

About My Writing

Name: _____ Date:

In looking at my _____

I did a great job on . . .	I need to work on . . .

High-Frequency Words for Bingo

again	my	day	take
she	soon	every	than
going	called	family	that
one	but	for	think
next	that	friend	time
with	house	gave	upon
not	for	going	very
think	may	good	way
look	good	he	went
much	time	her	were
will	family	here	what
around	many	him	where
more	him	his	who
went	play	house	why
than	now	if	will
also	into	into	win
other	little	like	with
way	here	little	won
like	each	look	work
her	always	made	would
after	friend	many	you
you	that	may	your
let	can	more	young
were	every	much	
boy	has	name	
what	take	next	
because	gave	not	
right	why	now	
very	of	of	
came	saw	one	
day	your	other	
out	said	play	
made	they	put	
big	name	right	
so	upon	she	
he	smal	so	
before	could	soon	

Writing Rubric

	DON'T GIVE UP! CHECK YOUR WORK.	HEY! YOU'RE ALMOST THERE. CONTINUE . . .	YES! THAT'S AMAZING.
PUNCTUATION MARKS	Be careful. You are missing punctuation marks.	You have some punctuation marks, BUT not all of them. Go back and check.	Great job! You remembered to put correct punctuation marks in the right places! Hooray!
SPACING	You wrote a good story. BUT you forgot to put spacing. Use your finger to put spacing after each word.	Good writing. Go back because in some places you forgot to put spacing.	What a perfect job. You did it! You really made sure that after each word you put spacing.
WORDS AND PICTURES . . . ARE THEY MATCHING?	We like your story. We like your picture. BUT they don't match.	We like your story. We like your picture. BUT there are some places or parts that don't make sense. Check your picture or writing or both.	We like your story. We like your picture. They match perfectly!
UPPER CASE AND LOWER CASE LETTERS	In your story/writing, you are using all uppercase letters or all lowercase letters or they are all mixed up. Go back and fix it with the magic tape.	You need to go back and make some changes because you are mixing up upper and lower case letters. Don't forget: the word *I* is always upper case.	You remembered to use upper- and lowercase letters correctly in your writing. You even remembered that the word *I* is always upper case.
SPELLING	You took chances by writing words in your own way.	You wrote some words in your own way. BUT you spelled some words like we would see in published books.	Wow! You really learned how to spell. Your words are like we would see in a dictionary or published books.
HANDWRITING	STOP scribbling! Take your time. Write your words so other people can read your writing.	Dont rush! Check the way you wrote some of your letters.	Your handwriting is beautiful. It is easy for other people to read your work.